Images
of the
Five Mile Woods Preserve

Images
of the
Five Mile Woods Preserve

Photographs by
Donald Formigli
Hank Miiller

Compiled by
Peter Osborne

Images of the Five Mile Woods Preserve
Photographs by
Donald Formigli and Hank Miiller
Compiled by
Peter Osborne

Published by
Heritage Conservancy
Doylestown, Pennsylvania

Copyright © 2017 by Heritage Conservancy

ISBN 978-0-692-91094-8 (soft cover)

Library of Congress Control Number: 2017910008

NATURE / Environmental Conservation & Protection
NATURE / Regional
NATURE / Ecosystems & Habitats / General
NATURE / Natural Resources
HISTORY / United States / State & Local / Middle Atlantic
(DC, DE, MD, NJ, NY, PA)

Cover and book design by Peter Osborne and The Wild Horse Creek Company

First Edition
10 9 8 7 6 5 4 3 2 1
Printed in the United States of America

Dedicated To

The visionaries who created the Five Mile Woods Preserve

and

Those who have continued on with its mission

Five Mile Woods in April
by
George Ivers
Presented to the people of Lower Makefield Township upon the approval of the referendum to purchase the Five Mile Woods in 1978.
Etching on paper, Limited edition
Used with the permission of Iris Ivers
Collection of Pat Miiller

Pink lady's-slipper
Cypripedium acaule
Flowers May–early July
1985
Donald Formigli

The Five Mile Woods
by
Lynn Sims

I walked last evening thru the quiet woods.
I saw the orchids rise above the leaves;
Watched the frogs leap o'er the stream,
and the deer go running through the green
Of the Five Mile Woods.

Oh why can't the orchids bloom forever.
Why can't the forest grow untouched.
But in the distance you can hear
The hammers and the dozers near.

There was a stream meandering upon its way
beside the trees reaching to the sky;
such lovely trees to walk beneath or
sit beneath or dream beneath,
now all concrete!

Oh rise ye sleeping people rise.
Oh speak ye silent people speak.
For then your words someone will hear,
And this woodland shall not disappear.

Then the orchids they shall bloom forever,
and the forest grow a century more,
and always there shall be this place
of solitude and subtle grace.
This Five Mile Woods.
This Five Mile Woods.

©Copyright 1978 by Lynn Sims
Reprinted with permission of the author

Contents

Foreword
Page 13

Introduction
Page 15

Herbaceous Plants
Page 19

Fungi
Page 61

Shrubs, Vines *and* Trees
Page 67

The Waters
Page 91

The Fall Line
Page 107

Art in the Woods
Page 115

Reflection, Solitude *and* Studying the Preserve
Page 143

Telling the Story
Page 165

SPECIES LISTINGS *and* RESOURCES
Page 179

ACKNOWLEDGEMENTS
Page 205

ABOUT THE PHOTOGRAPHERS *and* COMPILER
Page 209

COLOPHON
Page 216

Pink lady's-slipper
Cypripedium acaule
Flowers May-early July
1982
Hank Miiller

Foreword

This companion book to *The Five Mile Woods: A History* was conceived as the Woods history book was nearing completion. Peter and I were discussing how the book covered all the details of the Woods except for color photos which would have boosted the price more than we thought would be reasonable even if only were a few pages were included. We decided that a companion book of just color photos would be best.

Photography has been part of my life since I was very young. My father always took pictures and put them in albums all neatly lettered in white ink on the black album paper. I got started with a Brownie camera and never stopped clicking away, filling multiple albums and, later, cartons of color slides. I have hundreds of color slides taken in the Woods during the period of the 1970s when we were fighting to save it. All of my slides are now transferred to digital format. Some are better than others but with computer editing I was able to improve some of them. But to fill a whole book with really book quality photos, we needed to look beyond what I had. We were fortunate to be given the use of other photo collections primarily from Hank Miiller.

Some of the photos in this book show what existed in the 1970s and are no longer there. The Woods are an evolving system, changing the conditions available for various plant requirements to thrive. In the 1970s, there were more open areas where meadow plants grew. When these areas reverted to forest those plants died out. Also, it is likely that the exploding deer population in the Woods has caused some plants to disappear.

I hope this companion book of images will inspire readers to explore the Woods with their own cameras. Every season in the Five Mile Woods has opportunity for photography.

Don Formigli
Levittown, Pennsylvania
July 30, 2017

Introduction

The Five Mile Woods Preserve, located in Lower Makefield Township, Pennsylvania, is a remarkable place. Within its boundary is the only remaining section of the Fall Line in Pennsylvania that is undisturbed. This unique geological feature is the meeting point of the two ancient geologic regions, the Atlantic Coastal Plain Province and the Piedmont Province. It is also home to rare plants and an oak-beech forest.

The Preserve also makes for a great story. William Penn signed the patent that allowed an early Quaker settler to purchase the land in 1684. The families who lived there for more than two centuries were prosperous farmers. Visionaries saved the Woods from being developed for housing in the late 1970s and early 1980s. Because of those efforts, future generations of township residents will be able to enjoy this special place. In addition, the Preserve presents an excellent case study of land management over the last three centuries. It was farmed, used for pasture, timbered, and is now covered by a forest.

Much of this story was told in a four-hundred-page book entitled, *The Five Mile Woods: A History,* released in early 2017. When the book was finished, Don Formigli suggested that we might next focus on revealing the natural beauty of the Preserve through photographic images taken over the last five decades. Hence the birth of *Images of the Five Mile Woods Preserve*. This volume, a collection of more than one hundred and fifty color images, reveals the remarkable beauty of the Woods beginning in the late 1970s. As will be seen, many of the photographs were taken when efforts were underway to save the Woods from residential development.

This book is a testament to the remarkable and gifted photographic skills of Don Formigli and Hank Miiller. Over the years Don has entered a local nature center annual photo contest in the amateur category and has won second or third place ribbons in selected categories several times. Don's photograph of the *Yellow trout-lily* (page 26) appeared in the Heritage Conservancy's 2017 calendar. It was featured in the month of April.

Hank has been the recipient of many honors including first place ribbons and Best in the Show awards. Three of the award winning photographs are included here and entitled *Spring Trail* (page 133), *Summer Fern* (page 136), and *Woodland Slipper* (page 217).

Subjects include herbaceous plants, fungi, shrubs, vines, trees, the Queen Anne Creek, people enjoying and studying the Preserve and a chapter entitled *Art in the Woods*. The photographer's name and the date of the photograph is included in each caption. Some of the 1970s era photographs do not have the sharpness or clarity of the more recent photographs taken with digital cameras. However, we felt that they represented an important era in the Preserve's history.

Where possible, plants are identified by their common name and scientific name and use the same style and format as shown in the *Species Listings* at the end of this book. To more accurately identify the flora of the Woods, *The Plants of Pennsylvania: An Illustrated Manual* (Second Edition) by Ann Rhoads and Timothy Block was used. In addition, Dr. Rhoads was kind enough to review the individual captions. If a detailed identification was not possible, then a generic name is used. This volume is not meant to be a definitive guide to the plants in the Preserve as there are hundreds of species located within its boundaries.

The comprehensive *Species Listings* reflect the ongoing efforts to record the various species that can be found there. However, the inventories also demonstrate the fact that like all things in nature, change is constant. Species found decades ago are no longer present, and plants not located there in the 1970s, can now be found there.

We encourage you to take this book into the Woods, particularly in the late spring when so many of the plants, shrubs and trees bloom, and enjoy the amazing beauty of the Five Mile Woods Preserve.

Peter Osborne
Red Cloud, Nebraska
July 30, 2017

Herbaceous Plants

Pink lady's-slipper
Cypripedium acaule
Flowers May-early July
1977
Donald Formigli

Pink lady's-slipper
Cypripedium acaule
Flowers May-early July
1978
Donald Formigli

WHORLED-POGONIA
Isotria verticillata
Flowers late May-June
1978
Donald Formigli

WHORLED-POGONIA
Isotria verticillata
Flowers late May-June
1982
Hank Miiller

Soapwort gentian
Gentiana saponaria
Flowers September-October
1978
Donald Formigli

Soapwort gentian
Gentiana saponaria
Flowers September-October
1977
Donald Formigli

Yellow trout-lily
Erythronium americanum
Flowers April-May
2016
Donald Formigli

Yellow trout-lily
Erythronium americanum
Flowers April-May
1978
Donald Formigli

Nodding ladies' tresses
Spiranthes cernua
Flowers late July–October
1982
Donald Formigli

Celandine, lesser
Ranunculus ficaria
Flowers March-May
*This is a non-native, invasive exotic species and, as such,
is not native to the Five Mile Woods.*
2016
Donald Formigli

Dewberry
Rubus sp.
Flowers April-June, Fruit-June
2016
Peter Osborne

Rue anemone
Anemonella thalictroides
Flowers April-June
1978
Donald Formigli

Skunk-cabbage
Symplocarpus foetidus
Flowers February-April
1979
Hank Miiller

Skunk-cabbage
Symplocarpus foetidus
Flowers February-April
2016
Donald Formigli

Pipsissewa
Chimaphilla maculata
Flowers late June-July
1979
Donald Formigli

BELLWORT
Uvularia sessilifolia
Flowers April-May
1978
Donald Formigli

Beechdrops
Epifagus virginiana
Flowers July-October
1978
Donald Formigli

BLOODROOT
Sanguinaria canadensis
Flowers April-early May
1978
Donald Formigli

Springbeauty
Claytonia virginica
Flowers late March-early May
1978
Donald Formigli

BLUETS, QUAKER-LADIES
Houstonia caerulea
Flowers April-June
1978
Donald Formigli

Tall meadow-rue
Thalictrum pubescens
Flowers June-August
1978
Donald Formigli

Indian cucumber-root
Medeola virginiana
Flowers late May-early June
1978
Donald Formigli

AMERICAN BUGBANE
Actaea pachypoda
Flowers May-June
1978
Donald Formigli

American bugbane
Actaea pachypoda
Flowers May-June
1978
Donald Formigli

Enchanter's-nightshade
Circaea canadensis sp. Canadensis
(C. lutetiana, C. quadrisulcata)
Flowers June-August
1978
Donald Formigli

Downy rattlesnake-plantain
Goodyera pubescens
Flowers June-August
1978
Donald Formigli

Wool-grass
Scirpus cyperinus
Flowers June-September
1978
Donald Formigli

Dwarf ginseng
Panax trifolius
Flowers April-June, Fruit July-August
1979
Donald Formigli

Small white aster
Symphyotrichum racemosum (Aster vimineus)
Flowers August-October
1978
Donald Formigli

INDIAN-PIPE
Monotropa uniflora
Flowers late June-early August
1978
Donald Formigli

Common blue violet
Viola sororia var. sororia
Flowers March-June
1979
Donald Formigli

Swamp milkweed
Asclepias incarnata
Flowers June-August
1979
Donald Formigli

JACK-IN-THE-PULPIT
Arisaema triphyllum ssp. pusillum
Flowers late April-June
2016
Peter Osborne

JACK-IN-THE-PULPIT
Arisaema triphyllum ssp. pusillum
Flowers late April–June
1978
Donald Formigli

JACK-IN-THE-PULPIT
Arisaema triphyllum ssp. pusillum
Flowers late April-June
1979
Hank Miiller

JACK-IN-THE-PULPIT
Arisaema triphyllum ssp. pusillum
Flowers late April-June
1978
Donald Formigli

Mayapple
Podophyllum peltatum
Flowers May
1978
Donald Formigli

Mayapple
Podophyllum peltatum
Flowers May
1978
Donald Formigli

Fiddleheads
1978
Donald Formigli

Ferns
1978
Donald Formigli

FUNGI

Mushroom
1979
Donald Formigli

Stinkhorn mushroom
Phallus impudicus
1977
Donald Formigli

Bracket fungus
Polyporus versicolor
1978
Donald Formigli

Bracket fungus
Ganoderma tsugae
2009
Donald Formigli

Shrubs, Vines, *and* Trees

Highbush blueberry
Vaccinium corymbosum
Flowers May, Fruit July-August
1975
Donald Formigli

Highbush blueberry
Vaccinium corymbosum
Flowers May, Fruit July-August
1978
Donald Formigli

Blackhaw viburnum
Viburnum prunifolium
Flowers May, Fruit late July-September
1977
Donald Formigli

Pinxter-flower
Rhododendron periclymenoides
Flowers May
1978
Donald Formigli

Swamp azalea
Rhododendron viscosum
Flowers June
1978
Donald Formigli

Maple-leaved viburnum
Viburnum acerifolium
Flowers early June, Fruit September
1975
Donald Formigli

CRANBERRY
Vaccinium macrocarpon
Flowers June, Fruit September-October
1979
Donald Formigli

CRANBERRY
Vaccinium macrocarpon
Flowers June, Fruit September-October
1978
Donald Formigli

CRANBERRY
Vaccinium macrocarpon
Flowers June, Fruit September-October
1978
Donald Formigli

Acorn sprout
1978
Donald Formigli

Tree seedling
1978
Donald Formigli

Flowering dogwood
Cornus florida
Flowers early May, Fruit August-September
1978
Donald Formigli

Sweetgum
Liquidambar stryaciflua
Flowers late April
2017
Peter Osborne

AMERICAN BEECH
Fagus grandifolia
Flowers in April-early May as leaves unfold
2015
Donald Formigli

American beech
Fagus grandifolia
Flowers in April-early May as leaves unfold
2016
Donald Formigli

Maple leaf
1978
Donald Formigli

Scots pine
Pinus sylvestris
1979
Donald Formigli

Evergreen tree survivors from the Willard Nursery
2016
Donald Formigli

Winter in the Woods
1979
Donald Formigli

Crabapple
Malus sp.
1978
Donald Formigli

Gall
2016
Donald Formigli

Oak leaf gall
1979
Donald Formigli

The Waters

John Banko at the spring marking where the headwaters of the Queen Anne Creek once began north of Big Oak Road
1979
Donald Formigli

A channel of the Queen Anne Creek north of Big Oak Road
2016
Peter Osborne

The Queen Anne Creek as it enters the Preserve near Big Oak Road
2016
Peter Osborne

The Queen Anne Creek
2016
Donald Formigli

The Queen Anne Creek in the winter
1978
Donald Formigli

Frozen waters
1976
Donald Formigli

The Queen Anne Creek in Springtime
1979
Donald Formigli

Spring along the Queen Anne Creek
Green Frog (Rana (Lithobates) clamitans) and Springbeauty (Claytonia virginica)
2016
Donald Formigli

The Queen Anne Creek
2008
Donald Formigli

The Queen Anne Creek in the summer
2015
Donald Formigli

Vernal Pool in the western end of the Preserve
1977
Donald Formigli

Wetland near Big Oak Road
2016
Peter Osborne

Mossy bank in the northern end of the Preserve
1979
Donald Formigli

Vernal pool in the western end of the Preserve
1978
Donald Formigli

The Fall Line

The Fall Line
2016
Peter Osborne

Atop the Fall Line
1977
Donald Formigli

The Fall Line near Route 1
1975
Donald Formigli

Remains of an Eighteenth century quarry cut in the Fall Line
2016
Peter Osborne

Remains of a second quarry cut into the Fall Line
2017
Peter Osborne

The Queen Anne Creek passing through the Fall Line
2015
Donald Formigli

Art in the Woods

New Beginning
1980
Hank Miiller

Rising from a bed of moss
1979
Donald Formigli

Looking Skyward
2016
Donald Formigli

Crescent Fall Beauty
2009
Donald Formigli

Morning Dew
1980
Hank Miiller

Moth on a Fern
Clymene Moth (Haploa clymene)
2009
Donald Formigli

Fungi on a tree in the Woods
2015
Donald Formigli

The Woods in the fall
2016
Donald Formigli

One Mushroom
1983
Hank Miiller

CRYSTALS
1980
Hank Miiller

Along the bank of the Queen Anne Creek
2008
Donald Formigli

Tree bench
2009
Donald Formigli

Natural Patterns
1980
Hank Miiller

Winter in the Woods
1978
Donald Formigli

Woodland Ice
1982
Hank Miiller

Bird's nest under cover
1979
Donald Formigli

Spring Buds
New York ironweed (Vernonia Noveboracensis)
1982
Hank Miiller

Spring Trail
*May Apples (Podophyllum peltatum) and
Springbeauties (Claytonia virginica)*
1980
Hank Miiller

Reflections from the Queen Anne Creek
2016
Donald Formigli

Final Resting Place
Blue Jay feather (Cyanocitta cristata) and Springbeauties (Claytonia virginica)
2016
Donald Formigli

Summer Fern
1982
Hank Miiller

The frost will come soon
2016
Donald Formigli

Following the sun
2009
Donald Formigli

Big and Small
1980
Hank Miiller

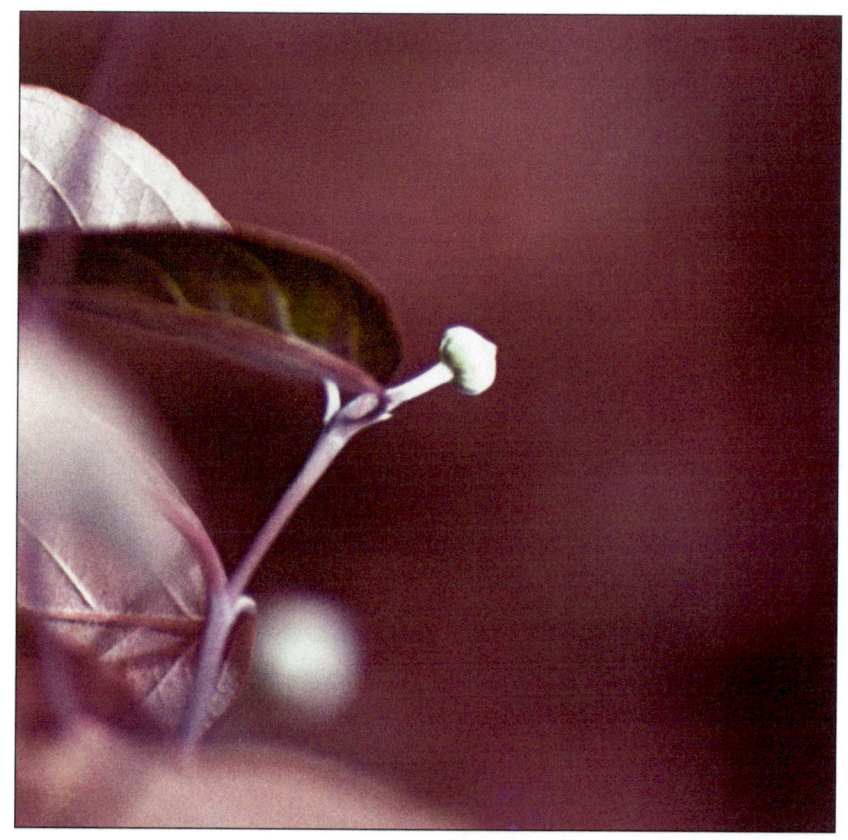

NEW LIFE
1980
Hank Miiller

Queen Anne
1980
Hank Miiller

Reflection, Solitude *and* Studying the Preserve

Solitude on the Queen Anne Creek
1979
Donald Formigli

Dr. Edgar Wherry exploring the Woods
1975
Donald Formigli

Observing the Queen Anne Creek
2008
Donald Formigli

Webelos Cub Scouts on a hike
1975
Donald Formigli

Finding a Box Turtle
Eastern Box Turtle (Terrapene carolina carolina)
1977
Donald Formigli

Family
2008
Donald Formigli

William and Morris Satterthwaite
Descendants of the early settlers at the family homestead
1978
Donald Formigli

Content on a winter day
Lynne Formigli and Friend
1979
Donald Formigli

Capturing the beauty of the Preserve
1978
Donald Formigli

Donald Formigli
The Patron Saint and Founder of
the Five Mile Woods Preserve
1977
Courtesy Donald Formigli

Pat (Fair) Miiller
Another visionary who created the Preserve
1978
Donald Formigli

Ann Rhoads and Gail Hardesty
Two of the visionaries who created the Preserve
1978
Donald Formigli

Congressman Peter Kostmayer (center) with aides
learning about the Five Mile Woods
1977
Donald Formigli

A WALK IN THE WOODS
1978
Donald Formigli

Cleaning up the Woods
1979
Donald Formigli

Picking berries at the cranberry bog
1979
Donald Formigli

CROSSING THE QUEEN ANNE CREEK
1978
Donald Formigli

Work Day at the Preserve
2016
Peter Osborne

Cutting brush at the Preserve's headquarters
2016
Peter Osborne

A TRAIL AWAITING A VOYAGE OF DISCOVERY
Sweetgum Trail
2009
Donald Formigli

Telling the Story

Remains of the chimney support foundation of the
William Dark, and later, the William Satterthwaite home
1978
Donald Formigli

Remains of the foundation of the William Dark and William Satterthwaite home almost forty years later showing signs of having deteriorated significantly
2016
Peter Osborne

Remains of a nineteenth century barn
near the Preserve's headquarters
2016
Peter Osborne

The Brelsford House
Late eighteenth century Bucks County stone house
2016
Peter Osborne

Remains of an old stone wall
2016
Peter Osborne

Researching the Five Mile Woods
John Lloyd and James Foulds
2016
Donald Formigli

Researching the Five Mile Woods
Peter Osborne and the venerable historian Sam Snipes
2017
Donald Formigli

Sharing the Natural Legacy of the Woods
John Lloyd, Chairman, Friends of the Five Mile Woods
2016
Peter Osborne

Earth Day with Jan McFarlan, former chairman of the Friends of the Five Mile Woods (left), talking with visitors
2016
Peter Osborne

Telling the story of the Woods
John Heilferty, Preserve Manager
2016
Peter Osborne

The Queen Anne Creek in Spring
1979
Donald Formigli

The Queen Anne Creek
by
Lynn Sims

In Five Mile Woods as rain drops fall,
around the trees.
From springs and bogs the channels form,
Moving through the deep.
Cross under roadway waters leap,
and so begins the Queen Anne Creek.

The water snakes a twisting path
in soil as hard as clay.
In places wide and narrow,
and under fallen tree.
Water swelling, rising, spreading,
beyond the bounds of the Queen Anne Creek.

Spring banks are lined with flowers,
baneberry, daisies and ferns,
bright trout lilies, pale spring beauty.
Jack-in-the-pulpit and violets too.
Summer shade brings bright green grasses,
in Five Mile Woods, the Queen Anne blue.

Onward, southward moves the stream,
rocky ravine cut deep.
Here the creek cuts through the fall
dropping fifty feet.
Deep within the Five Mile Woods,
a trail along the Queen Anne Creek.

©Copyright 1978 by Lynn Sims
Reprinted with permission of the author

Species Listings *and* Resources

The Five Mile Woods Preserve maintains a comprehensive digital listing of plants, trees, mammals, reptiles, amphibians and birds found there and in the greater Five Mile Woods area. These listings combine all the inventories previously created by Donald Formigli, Rick Mellon, John Heilferty, John Lloyd, David B. Long, Ann Rhoads, Edgar Wherry, the Bowman's Hill Wildflower Preserve and the Academy of Natural Sciences of Philadelphia. They can be found in the Preserve's archives and include the following:

The Flora of Bucks County, Walter Benner, 1932.
Plant Life Identified on Cutler Property, Donald Formigli, 1974
Notes from Dr. Edgar Wherry, 1975
Five Mile Woods, Lower Makefield and Falls Townships Bucks County,
    Pennsylvania: A Brief Summary of the Natural Features and a Proposal to
Protect the Area, Donald Formigli, 1975-76
Animal Life Five Mile Woods Preserve, Donald Formigli, 1976-1978
Rare Plants of Five Mile Woods and *Five Mile Woods (Bucks County*
    Pennsylvania) Revisited, Alfred Schuyler, 1978-79
Plant Life Identified in Five Mile Woods, Donald Formigli, 1978-1981
Master Plan for the Five Mile Woods Preserve, Rick Mellon, c. 1981
The Birds of Five Mile Woods, c. 1990s
Bowman's Hill Plant Stewardship Index Surveys, John H. Heilferty, 2009
The Birds of Five Mile Woods, David B. Long, 2013

These various inventories were created at different times, and some of the species listed may no longer be found at the Preserve or more generally in the Woods because of the steady changes in the landscape that have occurred during the last forty years. The listings include the common names and scientific names. As of 2003, there were seven plants, three animals and a plant community that were considered either endangered, threatened or rare.

Plant Species Listing

The plant species listing includes growth habitat; whether the species is native (N) to Pennsylvania, or introduced from outside the state (I); and state (ST) and Pennsylvania Biological Survey (PBS) status including whether it is endangered (PE), threatened (PT), rare (PR), extirpated (PX), tentatively undetermined because of a lack of data (TU) or under review for future listing (N). Additional information on the various statuses can be found on the Pennsylvania Natural Heritage Program's web page at *http://www.naturalheritage.state.pa.us/Species.aspx*

It should also be noted that the list of plants at the Preserve is not complete and research continues to be conducted.

Bird Species Listing

This list was compiled from source materials which varied regarding standards for species inclusion, and should therefore be considered a list of possible bird species that could inhabit the Five Mile Woods Preserve on a regular or seasonal basis. In addition, this list contains a number of species which might make only very brief appearances or fly-overs during east-coast migrations, might take refuge during severe storm events or might occur merely as *vagrants*.

Resources

Plants

Ann Rhoads and William Klein. 1993. *The Vascular Flora of Pennsylvania, Annotated Checklist and Atlas.* Philadelphia: American Philosophical Society.

Ann Rhoads and Timothy Block, 2007. *The Plants of Pennsylvania, An Illustrated Manual.* Second Edition. Philadelphia, Pennsylvania: University of Pennsylvania Press.

Benner, Walter. 1932. *The Flora of Bucks County.* Philadelphia: Published by the author.

Edgar Wherry, John Fogg and Herbert Wahl. 1979. *Atlas of the Flora of Pennsylvania.* Philadelphia, Pennsylvania: Morris Arboretum of the University of Pennsylvania.

Geology

Rhoads, Ann. 2003. *An Evaluation of sites representing the Fall Line Zone in the Mid Atlantic region for eligibility as a National Natural Landmark, Site Evaluated: Five Mile Woods.* Five Mile Woods Preserve.

Richards, Horace. 1956. *Geology of the Delaware Valley.* Philadelphia: Mineralogical Society of Pennsylvania.

Roberts, David. 1996. *A Field Guide to Geology: Eastern North America.* New York: Houghton Mifflin Company.

Management Plans

Five Mile Woods Preserve: Guide for Preservation. June 7, 1979.

Hobaugh, Maurice. 1978. *Woodland Management Plan for the Five Mile Woods.* Pottstown, Pennsylvania: Pennsylvania Department of Environmental Resources.

Mellon, Rick. 1981. *Master Plan for the Five Mile Woods Preserve.* Lower Makefield Township, Pennsylvania: Mellon Biological Services.

Fall in the Woods
2016
Donald Formigli

PLANTS

COMMON NAME	SCIENTIFIC NAME	GROWTH HABIT	N/I	ST	PBS
American beech	Fagus grandifolia	deciduous tree	N		
American chestnut	Castanea dentata	deciduous tree	N		
American elm	Ulmus americana	deciduous tree	N		
Apple	Malus pumila	deciduous tree	I		
Basswood	Tilia americana var. americana	deciduous tree	N		
Big-tooth aspen	Populus grandidentata	deciduous tree	N		
Bitternut hickory	Carya cordiformis	deciduous tree	N		
Black oak	Quercus velutina	deciduous tree	N		
Black or Sweet birch	Betula lenta	deciduous tree	N		
Black walnut	Juglans nigra	deciduous tree	N		
Black willow	Salix nigra	deciduous tree	N		
Choke cherry	Prunus virginiana	deciduous tree	N		
Crabapple	Malus sp.	deciduous tree	N/I		
Cucumber magnolia	Magnolia acuminata	deciduous tree	N		
Flowering dogwood	Cornus florida	deciduous tree	N		
Gray birch	Betula populifolia	deciduous tree	N		
Hornbeam; Ironwood	Carpinus caroliniana	deciduous tree	N		
Ironwood	Ostrya virginiana	deciduous tree	N		
Mockernut hickory	Carya tomentosa	deciduous tree	N		
Northern red oak	Quercus rubra	deciduous tree	N		
Peach	Prunus persica	deciduous tree	I		
Pear	Pyrus sp.	deciduous tree	I		

COMMON NAME	SCIENTIFIC NAME	GROWTH HABIT	N/I	ST	PBS
Persimmon	Diospyros virginiana	deciduous tree	N		
Pignut hickory	Carya glabra	deciduous tree	N		
Pin oak	Quercus palusrtris	deciduous tree	N		
Quaking aspen	Populus tremuloides	deciduous tree	N		
Red ash	Fraxinus pennsylvanica	deciduous tree	N		
Red maple	Acer rubrum var. rubrum	deciduous tree	N		
Sassafras	Sassafras albidum	deciduous tree	N		
Scarlet oak	Quercus coccinea	deciduous tree	N		
Shadbush	Amelanchier canadensis	deciduous tree	N		
Shagbark hickory	Carya ovata	deciduous tree	N		
Silver maple	Acer saccharinum	deciduous tree	I		
Sour cherry	Prunus cerasus	deciduous tree	I		
Sourgum, Blackgum, Tupelo	Nyssa sylvatica	deciduous tree	N		
Swamp white oak	Quercus bicolor	deciduous tree	N		
Sweet cherry	Prunus avium	deciduous tree	I		
Sweetgum	Liquidambar stryaciflua	deciduous tree	N		
Tuliptree	Liriodendron tulipifera	deciduous tree	N		
Umbrella-tree	Magnolia tripetala	deciduous tree	N	PT	PR
White ash	Fraxinus americana var. americana	deciduous tree	N		
White oak	Quercus alba	deciduous tree	N		
Wild black cherry	Prunus serotina	deciduous tree	N		
Willow oak	Quercus phellos	deciduous tree	N		
Yellow birch	Betula alleghaniensis	deciduous tree	N		

COMMON NAME	SCIENTIFIC NAME	GROWTH HABIT	N/I	ST	PBS
Sweetbay magnolia	Magnolia virginiana	semi-evergreen tree	N		
Norway spruce	Picea abies	evergreen tree	I		
Red cedar	Juniperus virginiana	evergreen tree	N		
Scots pine	Pinus sylvestris	evergreen tree	I		
Short-leaf pine	Pinus echinata	evergreen tree	I	N	PT
White pine	Pinus strobus	evergreen tree	N		
American elder	Sambucus canadensis	deciduous shrub	N		
American filbert or hazelnut	Corylus americana	deciduous shrub	N		
Amur honeysuckle	Lonicera maackii	deciduous shrub	I		
Black huckleberry	Gaylussacia baccata	deciduous shrub	N		
Black locust	Robinia pseudoacacia	deciduous shrub	N		
Black raspberry	Rubus occidentalis	deciduous shrub	N		
Blackhaw viburnum, blackhaw	Viburnum prunifolium	deciduous shrub	N		
Common blackberry	Rubus allegheniensis	deciduous shrub	N		
Dangleberry	Gaylussacia frondosa	deciduous shrub	N		
Deerberry	Vaccinium stamineum	deciduous shrub	N		
False indigo	Amorpha fruticosa	deciduous shrub	I		
Fetter-bush, Swamp dog-hobble	Leucothoe racemosa	deciduous shrub	N	TU	PR
Hearts-a-bursting, Strawberry-bush	Euonymus americanus	deciduous shrub	N		
Highbush blueberry	Vaccinium corymbosum	deciduous shrub	N		
Japanese barberry	Berberis thunbergii	deciduous shrub	I		
Linden viburnum	Viburnum dilatatum	deciduous shrub	N		

COMMON NAME	SCIENTIFIC NAME	GROWTH HABIT	N/I	ST	PBS
Lowbush blueberry	Vaccinium pallidum (V. pallidum)	deciduous shrub	N		
Maleberry	Lyonia ligustrina	deciduous shrub	N		
Maple-leaved viburnum	Viburnum acerifolium	deciduous shrub	N		
Meadow-sweet, Narrow-leaved Meadowsweet	Spiraea alba var alba	deciduous shrub	N		
Multiflora rose	Rosa multiflora	deciduous shrub	I		
Northern arrowwood	Viburnum recognitum	deciduous shrub	N		
Pinxter-flower	Rhododendron periclymenoides	deciduous shrub	N		
Possum-haw	Viburnum nudum	deciduous shrub	N	PE	PE
Purple chokeberry	Aronia prunifolia	deciduous shrub	N		
Pussy willow	Salix discolor	deciduous shrub	N		
Red chokeberry	Aronia arbutifolia	deciduous shrub	N		
Red choleberry	Photinia pyrifolia (Pyrus arbutifolia)	deciduous shrub	N		
Silky dogwood	Cornus amomum	deciduous shrub	N		
Smooth winterberry	Ilex laevigata	deciduous shrub	N		
Southern arrowwood	Viburnum dentatum	deciduous shrub	N		
Spicebush	Lindera benzoin	deciduous shrub	N		
Staggerbush	Lyonia mariana	deciduous shrub	N	PE	PE
Staghorn sumac	Rhus typhina	deciduous shrub	N		
Steeple-bush; Hardhack	Spiraea tomentosa	deciduous shrub	N		
Swamp azalea	Rhododendron viscosum	deciduous shrub	N		
Swamp rose	Rosa palustris	deciduous shrub	N		
Sweet pepperbush	Clethra alnifolia	deciduous shrub	N		
Winterberry holly, Black alder	Ilex verticillata	deciduous shrub	N		
Witch-hazel	Hamamelis virginiana	deciduous shrub	N		

COMMON NAME	SCIENTIFIC NAME	GROWTH HABIT	N/I	ST	PBS
Bayberry	Myrica pensylvanica	semi-evergreen shrub	N		
American holly	Ilex opaca	evergreen shrub	N	PT	PT
Cranberry	Vaccinium macrocarpon	evergreen shrub	N		
Mountain laurel	Kalmia latifolia	evergreen shrub	N		
Sheep laurel	Kalmia angustifolia	evergreen shrub	N		
Catbrier/ Glaucus Greenbrier	Smilax glauca	deciduous vine	N		
Fox grape	Vitis labrusca	deciduous vine	N		
Frost grape	Vitus vulpina	deciduous vine	N		
Hog peanut	Amphicarpaea bracteata	deciduous vine	N		
Poison-ivy	Toxicodendron radicans	deciduous vine	N		
Swamp dewberry	Rubus hispidus	deciduous vine	N		
Virginia-creeper	Parthenocissus quinquefolia	deciduous vine	N		
Catbrier, Greenbrier	Smilax rotundifolia	semi-evergreen vine	N		
Japanese honeysuckle	Lonicera japonica	semi-evergreen vine	I		
American bugbane	Actaea pachypoda	herbaceous	N		
American germander	Teucrium canadense	herbaceous	N		
Annual bluegrass	Poa annua	herbaceous	I		
Appalachian ironweed, Tawny ironweed	Vernonia glauca	herbaceous	N	PE	PE
Appalachian sedge	Carex appalachica	herbaceous	N		

COMMON NAME	SCIENTIFIC NAME	GROWTH HABIT	N/I	ST	PBS
Arrow-leaved tearthumb	Polygonum sagittatum	herbaceous	N		
Asiatic dayflower	Commelina communis var. communis	herbaceous	I		
Awlfruit sedge	Carex stipata	herbaceous	N		
Barnyard-grass, cockspur	Echinchloa muricata (E. pungens)	herbaceous	N		
Bartonia	Bartonia virginica	herbaceous	N		
Bedstraw, cleavers	Galium aparine	herbaceous	N		
Bee-balm, Oswego-tea	Monarda didyma	herbaceous	N		
Beechdrops	Epifagus virginiana	herbaceous	N		
Beggar's-lice; virginia stickseed	Hackelia virginiana	herbaceous	N		
Bellwort	Uvularia sessilifolia	herbaceous	N		
Bitter dock	Rumex obtusifolius	herbaceous	I		
Bittersweet, Oriental; Asian	Celastrus orbiculatus	herbaceous	I		
Black cohosh, Black snakeroot	Actaea racemosa (Cimicifuga racemosa)	herbaceous	N		
Bladder sedge	Carex intumescens	herbaceous	N		
Bladdernut	Staphylea trifolia	herbaceous	N		
Bloodroot	Sanguinaria canadensis	herbaceous	N		
Blue marsh violet	Viola cucullata	herbaceous	N		
Blue vervain, Simpler's-joy	Verbena hastata	herbaceous	N		
Blue wood aster	Symphyotrichum cordifolium	herbaceous	N		
Bluets, Quaker-ladies	Houstonia caerulea	herbaceous	N		
Boneset	Eupatorium perfoliatum	herbaceous	N		
Broad beech fern	Thelypteris hexagonoptera (Dryopteris hexagonoptera)	herbaceous	N		
Broad looseflower sedge	Carex laxiflora	herbaceous	N		
Broad-leaf sedge	Carex platyphylla	herbaceous	N		

COMMON NAME	SCIENTIFIC NAME	GROWTH HABIT	N/I	ST	PBS
Brome-like sedge	Carex bromoides	herbaceous	N		
Broom-sedge	Andropogon glomeratus	herbaceous	N		
Broom-sedge	Andropogon virginicus	herbaceous	N		
Bugleweed	Lycopus virginicus	herbaceous	N		
Bull thistle	Cirsium vulgare	herbaceous	I		
Bur-reed	Sparganium americanum	herbaceous	N		
Button sedge	Carex bullata	herbaceous	N		
Calico aster	Symphyotrichum lateriflorum	herbaceous	N		
Canada goldenrod	Solidago canadensis	herbaceous	N		
Canada mayflower	Maianthemum canadense	herbaceous	N		
Canada thistle	Cirsium arvense var. arvense	herbaceous	I		
Canadian sanicle/Canada black snakeroot	Sanicula canadensis	herbaceous	N		
Canadian St. John's-wort	Hypericum canadense	herbaceous	N		
Cardinal-flower	Lobelia cardinalis	herbaceous	N		
Carrion-flower	Smilax herbacea	herbaceous	N		
Celandine, lesser	Ranunculus ficaria	herbaceous	I		
Christmas fern	Polystichum acrostichoides	herbaceous	N		
Cinnamon fern	Osmunda cinnamomea	herbaceous	N		
Clearweed	Pilea pumila	herbaceous	N		
Common blue violet	Viola sororia var. sororia	herbaceous	N		
Common burdock	Arctium minus	herbaceous	I		
Common dandelion	Taraxacum officinale	herbaceous	I		
Common milkweed	Asclepias syriaca	herbaceous	N		
Common mouse-ear chickweed	Cerastium vulgatum	herbaceous	I		

COMMON NAME	SCIENTIFIC NAME	GROWTH HABIT	N/I	ST	PBS
Common periwinkle	Vinca minor	herbaceous	I		
Common plantain	Plantago major	herbaceous	I		
Common wintercress	Barbarea vulgaris var. vulgaris	herbaceous	I		
Common woodrush	Luzula echinata	herbaceous	N		
Common yellow wood-sorrel	Oxalis stricta	herbaceous	N		
Cranefly orchid	Tipularia discolor	herbaceous	N	PR	
Creeping Bent-grass	Agrostis stolonifera	herbaceous	n/a		
Curly dock	Rumex crispus	herbaceous	I		
Cutgrass/White grass	Leersia virginica	herbaceous	N		
Cut-leaved grape fern	Botrychium dissectum	herbaceous	N		
Cypress Panic-grass	Dichanthelium dichotomum var. dichotomum	herbaceous	n/a		
Downy rattlesnake-plantain	Goodyera pubescens	herbaceous	N		
Dryspke sedge	Carex siccata	herbaceous	N		
Dwarf cinquefoil	Potentilla canadensis	herbaceous	N		
Dwarf dandelion	Krigia biflora	herbaceous	N		
Dwarf ginseng	Panax trifolius	herbaceous	N		
Early goldenrod	Solidago juncea	herbaceous	N		
Eastern narrowleaf sedge	Carex amphibola	herbaceous	N		
Eastern star sedge	Carex radiata	herbaceous	N		
Eastern straw sedge	Carex straminea	herbaceous	N		
Eastern woodland sedge	Carex blanda	herbaceous	N		
Ebony spleenwort	Asplenium platyneuron	herbaceous	N		
Emmons' sedge	Carex albicans var. emmonsii	herbaceous	n/a		
Enchanter's-nightshade	Circaea canadensis sp. Canadensis (C. lutetiana, C. quadrisulcata)	herbaceous	N		

COMMON NAME	SCIENTIFIC NAME	GROWTH HABIT	N/I	ST	PBS
Evening-primrose	Oenothera biennis	herbaceous	N		
False foxglove	Agalinus purpurea (Gerardia purpurea)	herbaceous	N		
False hellebore	Veratrum viride	herbaceous	N		
False nettle	Boehmeria cylindrica var. cylindrica	herbaceous	N		
False solomon's seal; Solomon's plume	Smilacina racemosa	herbaceous	N		
Field garlic	Allium vineale	herbaceous	I		
Field thistle	Cirsium discolor	herbaceous	N		
Field woodrush	Luzula multiflora	herbaceous	N		
Fireweed; Pilewort	Erechtites hieracifolia	herbaceous	N		
Forked rush	Juncus dichotomus	herbaceous	N	PE	PE
Fowl mannagrass	Glyceria striata	herbaceous	N		
Fox sedge	Carex vulpinoidea	herbaceous	N		
Gall-of-the-earth	Prenanthes trifoliata	herbaceous	N		
Graceful sedge	Carex gracillima	herbaceous	N		
Grass rush	Juncus biflorus	herbaceous	N	TU	PR
Grass-leaved goldenrod	Euthamia graminifolia var. graminifolia	herbaceous	N		
Gray goldenrod	Solidago nemoralis	herbaceous	N		
Greenwhite sedge	Carex albolutescens	herbaceous	N		
Ground ivy	Glechoma hederacea	herbaceous	I		
Hairgrass	Agrostis hyemalis	herbaceous	I		
Hairgrass/Long-awned Hair-grass	Muhlenbergia capillaris	herbaceous	N	PX	PX
Hairy bittercress	Cardamine hirsuta	herbaceous	I		
Halberd-leaf tearthumb	Persicaria arifolia	herbaceous	N		
Halberd-leaved tearthumb	Polygonum arifolium	herbaceous	N		

COMMON NAME	SCIENTIFIC NAME	GROWTH HABIT	N/I	ST	PBS
Hawkweed	Hieracium scabrum	herbaceous	N		
Hay-scented fern	Dennsteadtia punctilobula	herbaceous	N		
Heal-all, Self-heal	Prunella vulgaris var. lanceolata	herbaceous	N		
Heath aster	Symphyotrichum pilosum	herbaceous	N		
Henbit	Lamium amplexicaule	herbaceous	I		
Hoary tick-trefoil	Desmodium canescens	herbaceous	N		
Hollow Joe-pye-weed	Eurrochium fistulosum	herbaceous	N		
Hooked crowfoot	Ranunculus recurvatus	herbaceous	N		
Horse-balm, stoneroot	Collinsonia canadensis	herbaceous	N		
Hyssop skullcap	Scutellaria integrifolia	herbaceous	N		
Indian cucumber-root	Medeola virginiana	herbaceous	N		
Indian strawberry	Duchesnea indica	herbaceous	I		
Indian-hemp	Apocynum cannabinum	herbaceous	N		
Indian-pipe	Monotropa uniflora	herbaceous	N		
Indian-tobacco	Lobelia inflata	herbaceous	N		
Interrupted fern	Osmunda claytoniana	herbaceous	N		
Jack-in-the-pulpit	Arisaema triphyllum ssp. pusillum	herbaceous	N		
Jack-in-the-pulpit	Arisaema triphyllum ssp. triphyllum	herbaceous	N		
Japanese knotweed	Fallopia japonica	herbaceous	I		
Japanese stiltgrass	Microstegium vimineum	herbaceous	I		
Jewelweed; Touch-me-not	Impatiens capensis	herbaceous	N		
Jumpseed	Persicaria virginica	herbaceous	N		
Lady fern	Athyrium filix-femina var. angustum	herbaceous	N		
Lance-leaved violet	Viola lanceolata var. lanceolata	herbaceous	N		

COMMON NAME	SCIENTIFIC NAME	GROWTH HABIT	N/I	ST	PBS
Lemon-balm	Melissa officinalis	herbaceous	I		
Little bluestem	Schizachyrium scoparium	herbaceous	N		
Long sedge	Carex folliculata	herbaceous	N		
Long-leaved panic grass	Panicum longifolium	herbaceous	N	TU	PE
Low smartweed	Persicaria longiseta	herbaceous	I		
Mad-dog skullcap	Scutellaria lateriflora	herbaceous	N		
marsh bedstraw, cleavers	Galium obtusum	herbaceous	N		
Marsh fern	Thelypteris palustris	herbaceous	N		
Maryland meadow-beauty	Rhexia mariana	herbaceous	n/a		
Massachusetts fern	Thelypteris simulata	herbaceous	n/a		
Mayapple	Podophyllum peltatum	herbaceous	N		
Meadow-beauty	Rhexia virginica	herbaceous	N		
Mild water-pepper, Water smartweed	Persicaria hydropiperoides	herbaceous	N		
Moneywort	Lysimachia nummularia	herbaceous	I		
Netted chain-fern	Woodwardia areolata	herbaceous	N	N	PR
New York fern	Thelypteris novaboracensis	herbaceous	N		
Northern bracken fern	Pteridium aquilinum	herbaceous	N		
Northern swamp or marsh buttercup	Ranunculus hispidus var. carietorum (R. caricetorum)	herbaceous	N		
Orange daylily	Hemerocallis fulva	herbaceous	I		
Orchard Grass	Dactylis glomerata	herbaceous	I		
Ox-eye daisy	Leucanthemum vulgare (Chrysanthemum leucanthemum)	herbaceous	I		
Panic grass	Dichanthelium meridionale	herbaceous	N		
Panicled aster	Symphyotrichum lanceolatum ssp. lanceolatum (Aster simplex)	herbaceous	N		
Parrtridgeberry	Mitchella repens	herbaceous	N		

COMMON NAME	SCIENTIFIC NAME	GROWTH HABIT	N/I	ST	PBS
Path rush	Juncus tenuis var. tenuis	herbaceous	N		
Pennsylvania sedge	Carex pensylvanica	herbaceous	N		
Perfoliate bellwort	Uvularia perfoliata	herbaceous	N		
Pink lady's-slipper	Cypripedium acaule	herbaceous	N		
Pipsissewa; Spotted wintergreen	Chimaphilla maculata	herbaceous	N		
Pokeweed	Phytolacca americana	herbaceous	I		
Poverty grass	Danthonia spicata	herbaceous	N		
Primrose violet	Viola primulifolia	herbaceous	N		
Purple-stemmed aster	Symphyotrichum puniceum	herbaceous	N		
Purpletop	Tridens flavus	herbaceous	N		
Queen Anne's-lace, wild carrot	Daucus carota	herbaceous	I		
Ragweed	Ambrosia artemisiifolia	herbaceous	N		
Rattlesnake fern	Botrichium virginianum	herbaceous	N		
Reed canary grass	Phalaris arundinacea	herbaceous	I		
Reedgrass	Calamagrostis cinnoides	herbaceous	N		
Reflexed sedge	Carex retroflexa	herbaceous	N		
Rice cut grass	Leersia oryzoides	herbaceous	N		
Round-leaved throughwort	Eupatorium rotundifolium	herbaceous	N		
Royal fern	Osmunda regalis	herbaceous	N		
Rue anemone	Anemonella thalictroides	herbaceous	N		
Sandplain yellow flax	Linum intercursum	herbaceous	N	PE	PE
Screwstem	Bartonia paniculata	herbaceous	N	N	PR
Sedge	Carex tribuloides	herbaceous	N		
Seedbox, False loosestrife	Ludwigia alternifolia	herbaceous	N		

COMMON NAME	SCIENTIFIC NAME	GROWTH HABIT	N/I	ST	PBS
Sensitive fern	Onoclea sensibilis	herbaceous	N		
Shallow sedge	Carex lurida	herbaceous	N		
Shinleaf	Pyrola elliptica	herbaceous	N		
Short-hair sedge	Carex crinita var. crinita	herbaceous	N		
Silver-rod, White goldenrod	Solidago bicolor	herbaceous	N		
Skunk-cabbage	Symplocarpus foetidus	herbaceous	N		
Slender woodland sedge	Carex digitalis	herbaceous	N		
Small white aster	Symphyotrichum racemosum (Aster vimineus)	herbaceous	N		
Small-flowered crowfoot	Ranunculus abortivus	herbaceous	N		
Small-headed beak-rush	Rhynchospora capitellata	herbaceous	N		
Small-leaved Panic-grass	Dichanthelium dichotomum var. ensifolium	herbaceous	n/a		
Soapwort gentian	Gentiana saponaria	herbaceous	N	TU	PE
Soft rush	Juncus effusus var. Pylaei	herbaceous	N		
Soft rush	Juncus effusus var. solutus	herbaceous	N		
Solomon's-seal	Polygonatum biflorum	herbaceous	N		
Solomon's-seal	Polygonatum pubescens	herbaceous	N		
Southern beech fern	Phegopteris hexagonoptera	herbaceous	N		
Southern lady fern	Athyrium filix-femina var. asplenioides	herbaceous	N		
Southern yellow wood-sorrel	Oxalis dillenii ssp. filipes	herbaceous	N		
Spike-rush	Eleocharis tenuis var. tenuis	herbaceous	N		
Spotted St. John's-wort	Hypericum punctatum	herbaceous	N		
Spreading sedge	Carex laxiculmis var. laxiculmis	herbaceous	N		
Springbeauty	Claytonia virginica	herbaceous	N		
Star-flower	Trientalis borealis	herbaceous	N		

COMMON NAME	SCIENTIFIC NAME	GROWTH HABIT	N/I	ST	PBS
Sundrops	Oenothera fruticosa	herbaceous	N		
Swamp milkweed	Asclepias incarnata	herbaceous	N		
Swan's sedge	Carex swanii	herbaceous	N		
Sweet everlasting	Pseudognaphalium obtusifolium	herbaceous	n/a		
Sweet white violet	Viola macloskeyi	herbaceous	N		
Sweet-scented bedstraw	Gallium triflorum	herbaceous	N		
Tall meadow-rue	Thalictrum pubescens	herbaceous	N		
Tearthumb, Scratch-grass	Persicaria sagittata	herbaceous	N		
Thicket sedge	Carex abscondita	herbaceous	N		
Tickseed sunflower	Bidens polylepis	herbaceous	I		
Tickseed sunflower	Bidens trichosperma (Bidens cronata)	herbaceous	N		
Timothy	Phleum pratense	herbaceous	I		
Toothed wood fern	Dryopteris carthusiana	herbaceous	N		
Turtlehead	Chelone glabra	herbaceous	N		
Violet wood-sorrel	Oxalis violacea	herbaceous	N		
Water starwort, Water chick-weed	Callitriche stagnalis	herbaceous	N		
Water-plantain	Alisma triviale	herbaceous	N		
Weak rush	Juncus debilis	herbaceous	N	N	PT
White avens	Geum canadense var. canadense	herbaceous	N		
White snakeroot	Ageratina altissima	herbaceous	N		
White vervain	Verbena urticifolia	herbaceous	N		
White wood aster	Eurybia divaricata	herbaceous	N		
White-edged sedge	Carex debilis var. debilis	herbaceous	N		
Whorled loosestrife	Lysimachia quadrifolia	herbaceous	N		

COMMON NAME	SCIENTIFIC NAME	GROWTH HABIT	N/I	ST	PBS
Whorled-pogonia	Isotria verticillata	herbaceous	N		
Wild licorice	Gallium circaezans var. circaezans	herbaceous	N		
Wild licorice/Lance-leaved Wild Licorice	Gallium lanceolatum	herbaceous	N		
Wild sarsaparilla	Aralia nudicaulis	herbaceous	N		
Wild strawberry	Fragaria virginiana	herbaceous	N		
Wood anemone	Anemone quinquefolia	herbaceous	N		
Wood lily	Lilium philadelphicum	herbaceous	N		
Wood reedgrass	Cinna arundinacea	herbaceous	N		
Wool-grass	Scirpus cyperinus	herbaceous	N		
Wool-grass	Scirpus rubricosus (see Scirpus cyperinus)	herbaceous	N		
Wrinkle-leaf goldenrod	Solidago rugosa	herbaceous	N		
Yarrow	Achillea millefolium	herbaceous	I		
Yellow flax	Linum medium	herbaceous	N		
Yellow Foxtail	Setaria glauca	herbaceous	n/a		
Yellow star-grass	Hypoxis hirsuta	herbaceous	N		
Yellow trout-lily	Erythronium americanum	herbaceous	N		
Deep-rooted running-pine (clubmoss)	Lycopodium tristachyum	clubmoss	N		
Flat-branched ground-pine (clubmoss)	Lycopodium obscurum	clubmoss	N		
Northern running-pine (clubmoss)	Lycopodium complanatum	clubmoss	N		
Running-pine (clubmoss)	Diphasiastrum digitatum	clubmoss	N		
Lesser duckweed	Lemna minor	aquatic plant	N		

REPTILES

COMMON NAME	SCIENTIFIC NAME
Black Rat Snake	Elaphe obsoleta obsoleta
Box Turtle	Terrapene carolina
Eastern Box Turtle	Terrapene carolina carolina
Eastern Garter Snake	Thamnophis sirtalis sirtalis
Eastern Milk Snake	Lampropeltis triangulum triangulum
Northern Black Racer	Coluber constrictor constrictor
Northern Water Snake	Natrix sipedon
Spotted Turtle	Clemmys guttata

AMPHIBIANS

COMMON NAME	SCIENTIFIC NAME
American Toad	Anaxyrus americanus
Bullfrog	Lithobates catesbeianus
Eastern Redback Salamander	Plethodon cinereus
Green Frog	Lithobates clamitans
Northern Dusky Salamander	Desmognathus fuscus
Northern Red Salamander	Pseudotriton r. ruber
Northern Slimy Salamander	Plethodon glutinosus
Northern Spring Peeper	Pseudacris crucifer
Northern Two-lined Salamander	Eurycea bislineata
Spotted Salamander	Ambystoma maculatum
Wood Frog	Lithobates sylvaticus

MAMMALS

COMMON NAME	SCIENTIFIC NAME
Big Brown Bat	Eptisicus fuss
Eastern Cottontail Rabbit	Sylvilagus floridanus
Eastern Coyote	Canis latrans
Eastern Gray Squirrel	Sciurus carolinensis
Eastern Mole	Scalopus aquaticus
Eastern Red bat	Lasiurus borealis
Gray Fox	Urocyon cinereoargenteus
Hoary Bat	Lasiurus cinereus
Least Shrew	Cryptotis parva
Little Brown Myotis	Myotis lucifufus
Long-tailed Weasel	Mustela frenata
Meadow Vole	Microtus pennsylvanicus
Muskrat	Ondatra zibethica
Northern Flying Squirrel	Glaucomys sabrinus
Opossum	Didelphis marsupialis
Racoon	Procyon lotor
Red Fox	Vuples fulva
Short-tailed Shrew	Blarina brevicaudata
Silver-haired Bat	Lasionycteris noctivagans
Starnose Mole	Condulura cristata
Striped Skunk	Mephitis mephitis
White-footed Mouse	Peromyscus leucopus
Whitetail Deer	Sylvilagus floridanus
	Odocoileaus virginianus

BIRDS

COMMON NAME	SCIENTIFIC NAME
Acadian Flycatcher	Empidonax virescens
Alder Flycatcher	Empidonax alnorun
American Bittern	Botaurus lentigenosis
American Crow	Corvus brachyrhynchos
American Goldfinch	Spinus tristis
American Kestrel	Falco sparvernius
American Redstart	Setophaga ruticilla
American Robin	Turdus migratorius
American Tree Sparrow	Spizella arborea
American Woodcock	Philohela minor
American Woodcock	Scolopax minor
Bald Eagle	Haliaeetus leucocephalus
Baltimore Oriole	Icterus galbula
Bank Swallow	Riparia riparia
Barn Swallow	Hirundo rustica
Barred Owl	Strix varia
Bay-breasted Warbler	Dendroica castanea
Belted Kingfisher	Megaceryle alcyon
Bicknell's Thrush	Cathrarus bicknelle
Black Vulture	Coragyps atratus
Black-and-white Warbler	Mniotilta varia
Black-billed Cuckoo	Coccyzus erythropthalmust
Black-capped Chickadee	Parus atricapillus
Black-throated Blue Warbler	Setophaga caerulescens
Black-throated Green Warbler	Dendroica virens
Black-throated Warbler	Dendroica caerulescens
Blackburnian Warbler	Dendroica fuscus
Blackpoll Warbler	Dendroica striata
Blue Grosbeak	Passerina caerulea
Blue Jay	Cyanocitta cristata
Blue-gray Gnatcathcer	Polioptila caerulea
Blue-headed Vireo	Vereo solitarius
Blue-winged Warbler	Vermivora pinus
Broad-winged Hawk	Buteoe platypterus
Brown Creeper	Certha familiaris
Brown Thatcher	Toxostoma rufum

COMMON NAME	SCIENTIFIC NAME
Brown-headed Cowbird	Molothrus ater
Canada Goose	Branta Canadensis
Canada Warbler	Wilsonia candensis
Cape May Warbler	Dendroica tigrine
Carolina Chickadee	Parus carolinensis
Carolina Wren	Thryothorus ludovicianus
Cedar Waxwing	Bombycilla cedrorum
Cerulean Warbler	Setophaga cerulea
Chestnut-sided Warbler	Dendroica pansylvanica
Chimney Swift	Chaetura pelagica
Chipping Sparrow	Spizella passerine
Chuck-wills-widow	Caprimulus carolinensis
Cliff Swallow	Petrochelidon pyrrhonota
Common Flicker	Colaptes auratus
Common Grackle	Quiscalus quiscalus
Common Nighhawk	Chordeiles minor
Common Redpoll	Carduelis flammea
Common Yellowthroat	Geothlypis trichas
Cooper's Hawk	Accipiter cooperii
Dark-eyed Junco	Junco hyemalis
Downy Woodpecker	Picoides pubescens
Eastern Bluebird	Sialia sialis
Eastern Kingbird	Tyrannus tyrannus
Eastern Phoebe	Sayornis phoebe
Eastern Screech Owl	Megascops asio
Eastern Wood Pewee	Contopus virens
European Starling	Sternus vulgaris
Evening Grosbeak	Hesperiphona vespertina
Field Sparrow	Spizella pusilla
Fish Crow	Corvus ossifragus
Fox Sparrow	Passerella iliacia
Golden-crowned Kinglet	Regulus satrapa
Golden-winged Warbler	Vermivora chrysoptera
Goldfinch	Carduelis firstus
Gray Catbird	Dumetella carolinensis
Gray-cheeked Thrush	Catharus minimus

COMMON NAME	SCIENTIFIC NAME
Great Blue Heron	Ardea herodias
Great Crested Flycatcher	Myiarchus crinitus
Great Horned Owl	Bubo virginianus
Green Heron	Botaurus virescens
Hairy Woodpecker	Picoides villosus
Hermit Thrush	Catharus guttatus
Herring Gull	Larus argentatus
Hooded Warbler	Wilsonia citrina
House Finch	Carpodacus misicanus
House Sparrow	Passer domesticus
House Wren	Troglodytes aedon
Indigo Bunting	Passerina cyanea
Kentucky Warbler	Oporonis formosus
Killdeer	Chardarius vociferous
Least Flycatcher	Empidonax minimus
Lincoln's Sparrow	Melospiza lincolnii
Long-eared Owl	Asio otus
Louisiana Waterthrush	Seiurus motacilla
Magnolia Warbler	Dendroica magnolia
Mallard	Anas platyrhynchos
Mourning Dove	Zenaida macroura
Mourning Warbler	Oporonis philadelphica
Nashville Warbler	Vermivora ruficapilla
Northern Cardinal	Cardinalis cardinalis
Northern Flicker	Colaptes auratus
Northern Harrier	Circus cyaneus
Northern Mockingbird	Mimus polyglottos
Northern Parula Warbler	Parula Americana
Northern Waterthrush	Seiurus noveboracensis
Orchard Oriole	Icterus spurius
Osprey	Pandion halisaetus
Ovenbird	Seiurus aurocapillus
Palm Warbler	Dendroica palmarum
Pileated Woodpecker	Dryocopus pileatus
Pine Siskin	Carduelis pirius
Pine Warbler	Dendroica pinus

COMMON NAME	SCIENTIFIC NAME
Prairie Warbler	Dendroica discolor
Purple Finch	Carpodacus purpureus
Red-bellied Woodpecker	Melanerpes carolinus
Red-eyed Vireo	Vireo olivaceus
Red-headed Woodpecker	Melanerpes erythrocephalus
Red-shouldered Hawk	Buteo lineatus
Red-tailed Hawk	Buteo jamicaensis
Red-winged Blackbird	Agelaius phoeniceus
Ring-billed Gull	Larus delawarensis
Ring-necked Pheasant	Phasianus colchicus
Rose-breasted Grosbeak	Pheuctucus lodovicianus
Ruby-crowned Kinglet	Regulus calendula
Ruby-throated Hummingbird	Archilochus lolubris
Ruffed Grouse	Bonasa umbellus
Rufous-sided Towhee	Pipilo erythrophthalmus
Rusty Blackbird	Euphagus carolinus
Scarlet Tanager	Paraang loivcea
Sharp-shinned Hawk	Acceipiter striatus
Solitary Vireo	Vireo solitaries
Song Sparrow	Melospiza melodia
Swainson's Thrush	Catharus ustulatus
Swamp Sparrow	Melospiza georgiana
Tennessee Warbler	Vermivora peregrine
Tree Swallow	Tachycineta bicolor
Tufted Titmouse	Parus bicolor
Turkey Vulture	Cathartes aura
Veery	Cathraus fuscescens
Warbling Vireo	Vireo gilvus
White-breasted Nuthatch	Sitta carolinensis
White-crowned Sparrow	Zonotrichia leucophrys
White-eyed Vireo	Vireo griseus
White-throated Sparrow	Zonotrichia albicollis
Wild Turkey	Meleagris gallopavo
Willow Flycatcher	Empidonax traillii
Wilson's Warbler	Wilsonia pusilla
Winter Wren	Troglodytes troglodytes
Wood Duck	Aix sponsa

COMMON NAME	SCIENTIFIC NAME
Wood Thrush	Hylocichla mustelina
Worm-eating Warbler	Helmitheros vermivorus
Yellow Warbler	Dendroica petechia
Yellow-bellied Flycatcher	Empidonax flaviventris
Yellow-bellied Sapsucker	Sphyrapicus varius
Yellow-billed Cuckoo	Coccyzus americanus
Yellow-breasted Chat	Icteria virens
Yellow-rumped Warbler	Dendroica coronate
Yellow-throated Vireo	Vireo flavifrons

Fall Fern
1982
Hank Miiller

Acknowledgements

How can one express the necessary gratitude to Don Formigli for all that he did and continues to do for the Five Mile Woods Preserve? He was the visionary who began the effort four decades ago to save what was then the largest remaining forested area in lower Bucks County and a place of such geological significance. Don saw the effort through the various stages including creating a vision, finding support, raising awareness, helping to bring together an equally determined group of interested people, and seeking support from a diverse group of organizations, legislators, Township officials, botanists and volunteers. He gathered together the remarkable stars of the world of botany at the time to come and help create a groundswell of support.

In reading the minutes of the Township's Park and Recreation Board, one can only marvel at Don, and the dedication of his fellow board members, in attending meeting after meeting, dealing with a multitude of challenges simultaneously and bringing them to a successful conclusion. This was a critical moment in the Township's history, a one-time opportunity to guide the development process in a way that addressed quality-of-life issues. If they had not been willing to make great sacrifices at that moment the opportunity would have been lost forever.

On December 11, 1978, the first tract of land was purchased and the most significant acreage within the Five Mile Woods was set aside for future generations to enjoy. Then, three years later, the Preserve was officially dedicated. That would be an amazing accomplishment for most people, but Don did not cease his efforts. He also maintained a remarkable archive of photographs and manuscripts that tell the story of how the Preserve came to be created, and that document its fascinating plant life and geological wonders. He photographed events, recorded the various stages of the project, and supported its programs by giving of himself and inspiring others.

Finally, he commissioned this book and *The Five Mile Woods: A History* in 2017. He shared all his files with me and generously gave of his time. For this book he gave me access to the remarkable collection of photographs he has taken over the last four decades. It was hard to chose from the more than one thousand photographs that he had taken. Each was more beautiful than the last.

Don never told me what pictures to use, how to go about my job or how to interpret the materials he gave me. Aside from the creation of the Preserve, these books are perhaps his greatest gift because those efforts of long ago, and all the information that was found and compiled, will be saved for future generations. Staff, volunteers and visitors will be able to better understand the history, the geology, the flora and the beauty of the place that so many have worked hard to save.

We are very grateful to Hank Miiller, who was a Township Supervisor during the acquisition of the Woods, for his generosity. He played an important role in the creation of this book and was kind enough to convert the slides that he had taken of the Woods long ago into digital images. His photographs are remarkable works of art. Like Don, he was an important contributor to the saving of the Five Mile Woods all those years ago.

Dr. Ann Rhoads, an early supporter of the Woods preservation project and nationally recognized botanist, provided important assistance as she identified plants and offered insights and ideas when we were first discussing the creation of the book. Her book, *The Plants of Pennsylvania, An Illustrated Manual* (2nd edition), coauthored with Timothy Block, was of great assistance, and is a remarkable professional accomplishment. We are grateful for her willingness to confirm identifications and correct those that were incorrect.

We are grateful to Lynn Sims Lang, the Bucks County Balladeer, for allowing us to reproduce her two ballads written for, and performed as part of, the successful effort to raise awareness and to save the Woods. Her *Bucks County Ballads* were recorded and are still available.

We are grateful for Jeff Marshall's help and also for the Heritage Conservancy's acceptance of the book as a gift from Donald Formigli and agreeing to publish and distribute it. This will allow for the book to live on long into the future.

Others who assisted include Preserve Manager John Heilferty, Friends of the Five Mile Woods Chairman John Lloyd, former Friends chairman Jan McFarlan, and Pat Miiller. Pat gave us so much help with the history book and allowed us to borrow her copy of the line drawing of the Five Mile Woods created by well-known area artist George Ivers and have it digitally reproduced here. Mr. Ivers presented it to Lower Makefield Township in 1978 to celebrate the purchase the first tract of land which became the Five Mile Woods Preserve. We are grateful to Iris Ivers, George's wife, for permission to use her late husband's drawing on the inside cover of the book. Canal Frame-Crafts Gallery, located in Washington Crossing, Pennsylvania, undertook all the necessary scanning work to accomplish this task.

I am also appreciative to the readers of the manuscript, although I take complete responsibility for any typos, mistakes or errors which remain as I am sure there are still some. They include: Don Formigli, Sue Gotta, Pat Miiller, John

Heilferty, Kathy Pasko, Jan McFarlan, John Lloyd, Hank Miiller, and Ann Rhoads. They were all kind enough to read the manuscript for correct identifications, mistakes, context and offered their insights.

My sister, Elizabeth, and her husband Gary Stenftennagel, provided lodging, good cheer and encouragement (along with their dog, Dakota and cat, Eleanor).

To all of those listed, unlisted and those who have passed on, we offer our sincere thanks for making this book possible and for saving the Five Mile Woods so long ago.

Peter Osborne
Red Cloud, Nebraska
July 30, 2017

About the Photographers

Donald Formigli

DONALD FORMIGLI WAS THE LEADER OF THE EFFORTS to save the Five Mile Woods. He served in the United States Army from 1958-60. Stationed at the Army Ballistic Missile Command at the Redstone Arsenal in Huntsville, Alabama he was assigned to a lab working on the Saturn rocket. Those were exciting years when the United States was in a space race with the Russians. When the Arsenal had an exhibit at the Alabama State Fair, he was assigned as one of the soldiers to man the exhibit.

In 1967, Formigli moved into a house on Forrest Road, in Lower Makefield Township with his wife Ursula, and their children, Brent and Lynne. Having worked his way up to the position of General Foreman at U.S. Steel's Trenton Rope Mill, he went on to become a Sales Engineer. The mill was sold to Bridon American Corporation in 1984. Formigli retired from Bridon two years later to pursue a career in the financial services sector.

At the time, Formigli had many interests including wild plants, botany, gardening and, most notably, the general quality of life in the community in which he lived. From those interests came a passion for the Five Mile Woods which was located close to where he lived. Because the Woods was then privately owned, he would park his car along Big Oak Road and walk into the large tract and began to explore. As he did, he discovered a remarkable world of rare plants, fascinating geology and a place of solitude. He often took family members and friends there for hikes.

After he moved to Lower Makefield, he began attending Planning Commission meetings that focused on the Township's open space and recreation needs. Soon he realized the Township was not addressing those pressing concerns. He also knew development could not be legally stopped, it could only be managed. As a result of listening to the discussions at those meetings, Donald created an ad-hoc Lower Makefield Open Space Committee and served as its president. He designed the Township's *Bikeway Master Plan* and participated in tree surveys, including one undertaken in 1979 by the Bucks County Conservancy to inventory

Don Formigli
2017
Peter Osborne

trees that dated back to William Penn's time.

His interests to help the community led to an appointment to serve on the Lower Makefield Park and Recreation Board in 1973-74. He became its chairman in 1975, and served in that position until 1980. He also served on the Save Our Woods Committee. Active in the Republican party, he was a member of the Republican Club and in 1979, Formigli was elected to the Township's Board of Supervisors. He later served on the board of directors of Open Space, Inc, a not-for-profit dedicated to preserving Bucks County's rural landscape.

The Five Miles Woods preservation effort required a major commitment of time and effort and would not conclude until almost seven years later when the Five Mile Woods Preserve was dedicated in the fall of 1981. By that time, he had moved out of the Township.

Most of the Five Mile Woods came to be preserved either by purchase, or by the use of planning tools available at the time. It was Donald Formigli and his vision, more than any other single individual, who was responsible for this remarkable achievement. To be sure, there were many other supporters, and people who volunteered to help along the way, including other members of the Open Space Committee and the Save Our Woods Committee, Township officials, the solicitor and other organizations. However, if there is a patron saint of the Woods it is certainly Donald Formigli.

Over the years Don has entered a local nature center annual photo contest in the amateur category and has won second or third place ribbons in selected categories several times. His collection of photographs of the Five Mile Woods number at least one thousand images, and more than one hundred are featured in this book.

Hank Miiller

A unique style of natural spontaneity threads Hank's works. Commissioned works, especially children and adult portraits, often capture the expressive eye. Starting with a photography course in high school, and continuing through extensive business travels in Europe and the Far East, he has had the opportunity to photograph many unique subjects in Paris, Tokyo and Kyoto, Japan, and in Germany and Austria. Hank uses a high resolution, professional Nikon digital camera with selected lenses that produce excellent image renditions. Creative skills are applied with Adobe Photoshop.

Hank Miiller
2017
Hank Miiller

Exhibits
• In the Yardley, Pennsylvania area, his images have been displayed at the Yardley News, Yardley Jewelers, Wiedel Real Estate, the law offices of Kwasny, Reilly and Michaels, Yardley Travel, Canal Frame-Crafts Gallery, Washington Crossing, Pennsylvania, with the latter offering his art for sale.

• Participating in Bucks County Nature Center shows, his images have received Best in Show distinguishing awards, as well as a number of First Place ribbons.

• Selected nature images have been exhibited at Longwood Gardens.

• *The Crossing* and *Winter Crossing*, scenes associated with the Washington Crossing Historic Park, both received awards in juried art shows at Canal Frame-Crafts Gallery, Washington Crossing, Pennsylvania.

• A noted Yardley portrait painter acquired rights for several of Hank's images of New Orleans street entertainers to serve as a source for her portrait works.

Hank's commissioned works include images for magazine covers, portraits, and advertising for local companies.

About the Compiler

Peter Osborne

Peter Osborne is an independent historian, writer and lecturer who has worked in the public history field for more than thirty-five years. Born in Paterson, New Jersey, he holds a Bachelor of Arts degree from Rutgers, the State University of New Jersey. Osborne's professional interests include Theodore Roosevelt, Franklin and Eleanor Roosevelt, the state and national park systems, the Civilian Conservation Corps, and the famed Corps of Discovery Expedition led by Captains Meriwether Lewis and William Clark.

Osborne has been published widely over the last two decades. He has written four books on the Depression era and state parks including *We Can Take It! The Roosevelt Tree Army at High Point State Park 1933-1941*, *Images of America: High Point State Park and the Civilian Conservation Corps*, *Images of America: Hacklebarney and Voorhees State Parks (New Jersey)* and *Images of America: Promised Land State Park (Pennsylvania)*.

Between 2012 and 2014 he wrote a comprehensive two volume, twelve-hundred-page history about the state parks at the site of Washington's Crossing of the Delaware River. They were commissioned by William Farkas, president of Yardley Press of Yardley, Pennsylvania and entitled *Where Washington Once Led: A History of New Jersey's Washington Crossing State Park* and *No Spot In This Far Land Is More Immortalized: A History of Pennsylvania's Washington Crossing Historic Park*.

Over the years, Osborne has written about a variety of topics. In 2011, he co-authored *So Many Brave Men: A History of the Battle at Minisink Ford* with Mark Hendrickson and Jon Inners. In early 2016 he finished writing the first institutional history of the Commonwealth of Pennsylvania's official railroad museum. The book is entitled *The Trains of Our Memory: A History of the Railroad Museum of Pennsylvania 1965-2015*.

In 2017 he completed the first history ever written of the Five Mile Woods Preserve in Lower Makefield Township in southern Bucks County. The book told the remarkable story of the geological history of the three hundred acre natural area along with its history from its inhabitation by Native Americans, ownership by a number of Quaker families, and the efforts to save it from development in the late 1970s and early 1980s.

Osborne was the Executive Director of the Minisink Valley Historical Society in Port Jervis, New York, from 1981-2009, and the Port Jervis City Historian from 1989-2003. During his directorship, he was responsible for the Society's Fort Decker Museum of History. He then served as the Curator of Education and Special Events at the Red Mill Museum Village in Clinton, New Jersey from 2010-11. Since then he has been working as an independent historian and writer.

He owns the Wild Horse Creek Company and splits his time between Red Cloud, Nebraska and North Haledon, New Jersey. The mission of his company is to provide exciting journeys of discovery into our nation's history through presentations, lectures, demonstrations, motor coach tours and publications. The Wild Horse Creek Company (and its predecessor, the Pienpack Company) has been providing programs for civic, historical, fraternal, church groups, seminars, meetings, Elderhostel and Road Scholar programs for more than thirty-five years.

PETER OSBORNE
FOLLOWING THE TRAIL OF LEWIS AND CLARK AT THE LOLO PASS IN THE CLEARWATER NATIONAL FOREST IN WESTERN MONTANA.
2015

CONTACTING THE PHOTOGRAPHERS

The work of each of the photographers is available for purchase. Interested parties can contact them at the following addresses:

Hank Miiller
2203 Society Place, Newtown Pennsylvania 18940
Email: *hmiiller@earthlink.net*

Donald Formigli
455 Stonybrook Drive, Levittown, Pennsylvania 19055-2015
Email: *dformigli@aol.com*

CONTACTING THE COMPILER
Peter Osborne
Wild Horse Creek Company
819 North Seward Street, Red Cloud, Nebraska 68970
E-mail: *peter@wildhorsecreekcompany.com* or *peterosbornehistorian@gmail.com*
Web Page: *www.wildhorsecreekcompany.com*

ON THE FLOOR OF THE FOREST
2016
Donald Formigli

Colophon

The manuscript was prepared in Microsoft Word and transferred into Adobe InDesign CS4 for production. The book block was typeset in Adobe Garamond Pro. The cover was set in Trajan Pro and Adobe Garamond Pro. The paper used for the book block is White 70lb. The cover is four-color with a gloss film lamination and the book is perfect-bound. The cover and the book's interior design were created by Peter Osborne and the Wild Horse Creek Company. The book was then converted into a PDF and printed in the United States by Lightning Source, Inc. located in La Vergne, Tennessee. It was originally published by the Wild Horse Creek Company located in Red Cloud, Nebraska. The book is available for purchase directly from the Five Mile Woods Preserve, the Heritage Conservancy, local and regional book stores, and major online retailers including Barnes and Noble and Amazon.

The photograph used for the front cover was taken by Donald Formigli and is of several yellow trout lilies (*Erythronium americanum*) in bloom at the base of a American beech tree (*Fagus grandifolia)*. It was taken in the spring of 2016 and featured in the annual calendar in 2017 published by the Heritage Conservancy. The pictures used for the back cover of the book were also taken in the Preserve by Donald Formigli. The photograph of the flowering dogwood (*Cornus florida*) in bloom was taken in 1979 and the picture of the Queen Anne Creek was taken in 2008.

Woodland slipper
1977
Hank Miiller

www.ingramcontent.com/pod-product-compliance
Lightning Source LLC
Chambersburg PA
CBHW040912020526
44116CB00026B/38